KEEPSAKES

for the Heart

KEEPSAKES *for the Heart*

FAITH

Compiled by Alice Gray

Multnomah® Publishers—Sisters, Oregon

PRESENTED

to

God is able
God is able to do
God is able to do all
God is able to do all we ask
God is able to do all we ask or think
God is able to do beyond all we ask or think!

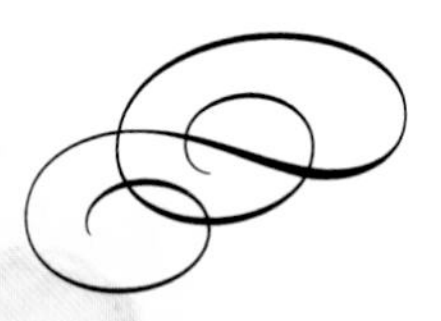

—Adapted from Ephesians 4:20

CONTENTS

Come Home!

Once there was a widow and her son who lived in a miserable attic. Years before, she had married against her parents' wishes and had gone with her husband to live in a foreign land.

He had proved irresponsible and unfaithful, and after a few years he died without having made any provision for her and the child. It was with the utmost difficulty that she managed to scrape together the bare necessities of life.

The happiest times in the child's life were those when the mother took him in her arms and told him about her father's house in the old country. She told him of the grassy lawn, the noble trees, the wild flowers, and the delicious meals.

The child had never seen his grandfather's home, but to him it was the most beautiful place in all the world....

One day the postman knocked at the attic door. The mother recognized the handwriting on the letter and with trembling fingers broke the seal. There was a check and a slip of paper with just two words: "Come Home."

Some day a similar experience will be ours—an experience shared by all who know Christ.... We do not know when the call will come. But some day a loving hand will be laid upon our shoulder and this brief message will be given: "Come Home."

All of us who know Christ personally need not be afraid to die. Death to the Christian is "going home."

—Billy Graham
from Unto the Hills

Sorrows

Have courage for the great sorrows of life
and patience for the small ones;
and when you have laboriously
accomplished your daily task,
go to sleep in peace.
God is *awake.*

—Victor Hugo

Even If it's Dark

He was a strong man facing an enemy beyond his strength.

His young wife had become gravely ill, then suddenly passed away, leaving the big man alone with a wide-eyed, flaxen-haired girl, not quite five years old.

The service in the village chapel was simple, and heavy with grief. After the burial at the small cemetery, the man's neighbors gathered around him. "Please, bring your little girl and stay with us for several days," someone said. "You shouldn't go back home just yet."

Broken-hearted though he was, the man answered, "Thank you, friends, for the kind offer. But we need to go back home—where she was. My baby and I must face this."

So they returned, the big man and his little girl, to what now seemed an empty, lifeless house. The man brought his daughter's little bed into his room, so they could face the first dark night together.

As the minutes slipped by that night, the young girl was having a dreadful time trying to sleep...and so was her father. What could pierce a man's heart deeper than a child sobbing for a mother who would never come back?

Long into the night the little one continued to weep. The big man reached down into her bed and tried to comfort her as best he could. After a while, the little girl managed to stop crying—but only out of sorrow for her father. Thinking his daughter was asleep, the father looked up and said brokenly, "I trust You, Father, but…it's as dark as midnight!"

Hearing her dad's prayer, the little girl began to cry again.

"I thought you were asleep, baby," he said.

"Papa, I did try. I was sorry for you. I did try. But—I couldn't go to sleep. Papa, did you ever know it could be so dark? Why Papa? I can't even see you, it's so dark." Then, through her tears, the little girl whispered, "But you love me even if it's dark—don't you, Papa? You love me even if I don't see you, don't you, Papa?"

For an answer, the big man reached across with his massive hands, lifted his little girl out of her bed, brought her over onto his chest, and held her, until at last she fell asleep.

When she was finally quiet, he began to pray. He took his little daughter's cry to him, and passed it up to God.

"Father, it's dark as midnight. I can't see You at all. But You love me, even when it's dark and I can't see, don't You?"

—Ron Mehl
from God Works the Night Shift

No Wasted Pieces

A tourist strolling through a European village stopped to observe a master craftsman of gold filigreed porcelain.

He watched as the craftsman took one of his loveliest pieces, an exquisite vase, and carefully examined it. After a few minutes, a faint smile of satisfaction touched the corners of the artist's mouth.

The workmanship was perfect; The size and form were just right; the artwork, intricate and delicate. Then, to the horror of the tourist, the craftsman picked up a hammer and smashed it into a thousand pieces.

"Why?" cried the stunned man when he finally retrieved his breath. "Why did you do that?"

The craftsman looked at the tourist and explained. "You see, my friends," he said, "the value of this vase is not in its perfection. Not in the artwork, not in its form or shape—as lovely as these may be. No, the value lies in the fact that I am now going to put these pieces back together again. With gold!"

So it is with our lives. The value of our lives lies not in our perceived perfections or lack of them...not in what we've done or left undone...not in how hard we've worked...not in our efforts, as sincere as they may be...not in the hope that we'll get a second chance to redeem ourselves. No, the value of our lives lies in the fact that God wastes nothing. He takes all the pieces of our lives, even the imperfect, shattered fragments, and puts them back together again with His blood, which is infinitely more precious than gold.

—*Gigi Graham Tchividjian*
from Currents of the Heart

The Treasure

The cheerful girl with bouncy golden curls was almost five. Waiting with her mother at the checkout stand, she saw them: a circle of glistening white pearls in a pink foil box.

"Oh please, Mommy. Can I have them? Please, Mommy, please!"

Quickly the mother checked the back of the little foil box and then looked back into the pleading blue eyes of her little girl's upturned face.

"A dollar ninety-five. That's almost two dollars. If you really want them, I'll think of some extra chores for you and in no time you can save enough money to buy them for yourself. Your birthday's only a week away and you might get another crisp dollar bill from Grandma."

As soon as Jenny got home, she emptied her penny bank and counted out seventeen pennies. After dinner, she did more than her share of chores and she went to the neighbor and asked Mrs. McJames if she could pick dandelions for ten cents. On her birthday, Grandma did give her another new dollar bill and at last she had enough money to buy the necklace.

Jenny loved her pearls. They made her feel dressed up and grown up. She wore them everywhere—Sunday school, kindergarten, even to bed. The only time she took them off is when she went swimming or had a bubble bath. Mother said if they got wet, they might turn her neck green.

Jenny had a very loving daddy and every night when she was ready for bed, he would stop whatever he was doing and come upstairs to read her a story. One night when he finished the story, he asked Jenny, "Do you love me?"

"Oh, yes, Daddy. You know that I love you."

"Then give me your pearls."

"Oh, Daddy, not my pearls. But you can have Princess—the white horse from my collection. The one with the pink tail. Remember, Daddy? The one you gave me. She's my favorite."

"That's okay, Honey. Daddy loves you. Good night." And he brushed her cheek with a kiss.

About a week later, after the story time, Jenny's daddy asked again, "Do you love me?"

"Daddy, you know I love you."

"Then give me your pearls."

"Oh, Daddy, not my pearls. But you can have my teddy bear. The brand new one I got for my birthday. She is so beautiful with her soft pink fur and matching ribbon"

"That's okay. Sleep well. God bless you, little one. Daddy loves you."

And as always, he brushed her cheek with a gentle kiss.

A few nights later when her daddy came in, Jenny was sitting on her bed with her legs crossed Indian-style. As he came close, he noticed her chin was trembling and one silent tear rolled down her cheek.

"What is it, Jenny? What's the matter?"

Jenny didn't say anything but lifted her little hand up to her daddy. And when she opened it, there was her little pearl necklace. With a little quiver, she finally said, "Here, Daddy. It's for you."

With tears gathering in his own eyes, Jenny's kind daddy reached out with one hand to take the dime-store necklace, and with the other hand he reached into his pocket and pulled out a blue velvet case with a strand of genuine pearls and gave them to Jenny. He had had them all the time. He was just waiting for her to give up the dime-store stuff so he could give her genuine treasure.

So like our heavenly Father.

—*Alice Gray*
from More Stories for the Heart

Never be afraid to trust
An unknown future
To a known God.

—Corrie ten Boom

The Father's Pleasure

Today the wind invited the children and me outside to chase it. So we did. The trees, like dancing gypsies with jewels in their hair laughed above us as we frolicked down the street. The pockets of my jacket began to fill with autumn treasures, placed there by two sets of small hands.

Returning to the warm house, red-faced and breathless, the children dumped their goodies onto the kitchen table, giddy with the joy of discovery. Along with several twigs and many rocks, Young Ross had bagged a snail's shell—minus one snail. Rachel laid out each of her big, amber-colored leaves, then chose the largest one to use as a fan. I watched them as they arranged and rearranged each acorn, rock, leaf, and twig, preparing their own centerpiece for the table. The children spoke in hushed tones, lost in wonder, mesmerized by a handful of God's trinkets.

It reminded me of when I was young. I would regularly bring home treasures to my mother and scatter them across the kitchen counter. One afternoon her hand passed over the tiny white pebbles and squashed red geraniums extracted from my pockets to stop at a tattered gray feather. I had almost left the spiny thing in the gutter since it appeared broken and useless.

Mom ran her fingers up the feather's tattered sides and turned it toward the kitchen window. Soft hues of sunshine lit the feather, changing it from dull gray to bright silvery-blue as she twirled it between her fingers, a marvelous wonder to my young eyes. An "ordinary" miracle.

With fumbling words I entered my children's moment of

wonder and told them how much God dearly treasured them. I wanted them to feel, in that moment, the pleasure of the Father, to understand how He delights in collecting the ordinary of this world and bringing it into the warmth of His kingdom. How His touch can turn the tattered into the dazzling.

Most of all, I wanted my children to know that their young hearts are not trinkets to be played with but are rare, priceless jewels in the hands of the King.

They looked at me with innocent eyes, nonplused by my intense lecture. Had I once looked at my own mother the same way?

Maybe such eternal truths can't really be taught, I decided. They can only be collected, examined, arranged, rearranged—and finally treasured. And this takes a lifetime of days filled with ordinary miracles.

—*Robin Jones Gunn*
from Mothering By Heart

Drifting

The story is told of a little boy who was floating his boat on a pond when the boat drifted away. A man came by, saw the boat drifting out on the pond, and began throwing stones on the far side of the boat. The boy asked, "What are you doing?" But then something very interesting happened. As the stones hit the water beyond the boat, they created ripples which pushed the boat back toward the boy. Even though the stones disturbed the smooth water, they achieved the desired result. That's how it is with God sometimes. When we drift away from Him, He throws the disturbing stones out beyond us in order to push us back to the shore of His love.

—*Tony Evans*

Do not have your concert first
and tune your instruments afterward.
Begin each day with God.

—James Hudson Taylor

Morning Song

I had been getting up early, fixing myself a cup of coffee, and then sitting in the rocker on the front porch while I prayed for each of our children, and for each of theirs.

One morning I awoke earlier than usual. It was five o'clock, with dawn just breaking over the mountains. I collected my cup of coffee and settled into the old rocker. Suddenly, I realized a symphony of bird song was literally surrounding me. The air was liquid with music, as if the whole creation were praising God at the beginning of a new day. I chuckled to hear the old turkey gobbler, that had recently joined our family, gobbling away down in the woods at the top of his voice as if he were a song sparrow!

And I learned a lesson. I had been beginning my days with petitions, and I should have been beginning them with praise.

—*Ruth Bell Graham*
from Legacy of a Pack Rat

I Am a Mother's Prayer

I am a mother's prayer: I am sometimes clothed in beautiful language that has been stitched together with the needles of love in the quiet chambers of the heart, and sometimes I am arrayed only in the halting phrases interrupted by tears which have been torn like living roots from the deep soil of human emotion. I am a frequent watcher of the night. I have often seen the dawn break over the hills and flood the valleys with light and the dew of the gardens has been shaken from my eyes as I waited and cried at the gates of God.

I am a mother's prayer: there is no language I cannot speak; and no barrier of race or color causes my feet to stumble. I am born before the child is born, and ere the day of deliverance comes, I have often stood at the altar of the Lord with the gift of an unborn life in my hands, blending my joyful and tearful voice with the prayers and tears of the father. I have rushed ahead of the nurse through the corridors of the hospital praying that the babe would be perfect, and I have sat dumb and mute in the presence of delight over a tiny bit of humanity, so overwhelmed I have been able to do nothing but strike my fingers on the harps of gratitude and say, "Well, thank the Lord!"

I am a mother's prayer: I have watched over the cradle; I have sustained a whole household while we waited for a doctor to come. I have mixed medicine and held up a thermometer that read 104°. I have sighed with relief over the sweat in the little one's curls because the crisis was past. I have stood by a graveside and picked a few flowers to take home like old memories, and cast my arms around the promises of God to just hang on and wait until I could feel underneath me the everlasting arms.

I am a mother's prayer: I have walked and knelt in every room of the house; I have fondled the old Book, sat quietly at the kitchen table, and been hurled around the world to follow a boy who went to war. I have sought through hospitals and army camps and battlefield. I have dogged the steps of sons and daughters in college and university, in the big city looking for a job. I have been in strange places, for I have even gone down into honky-tonks and dens of sin, into night clubs and saloons and back alleys and along dark streets. I have ridden in automobiles and planes and ships seeking and sheltering and guiding and reminding and tugging and pulling toward home and Heaven.

I am a mother's prayer: I have filled pantries with provision when the earthly provided was gone. I have sung songs in the night when there was nothing to sing about but the faithfulness of God. I have been pressed so close to the promises of the Word that the imprint of their truth is fragrant about me. I have lingered on the lips of the dying like a trembling melody echoed from Heaven.

I am a mother's prayer: I am not unanswered, although mother may be gone, although the home may be dissolved into dust, although the little marker in the graveyard grows dim. I am still here: and as long as God is God, and truth is truth, and the promises of God are "yes and amen," I will continue to woo and win and strive and plead with boys and girls whose mothers are in Glory, but whose ambassador I have been appointed by the King Emmanuel. I am a mother's prayer....

—Author unknown

Keep This for Me

"Keep this for me."
What child has not said this,
And placed a treasure in his Mother's hand
With strict injunction she should keep it safe
Till he return?
He knows with her it will be safe;
No troubled thought or anxious fear besets his mind.
And off he runs lighthearted to his play.

If children can so trust, why cannot we,
And place our treasures, too, in God's safe hand;
Our hopes, ambitions,
needs, and those we love,
Just see them, in His
all-embracing care,
And say with joyous heart,
"Keep these for me."

—Author unknown

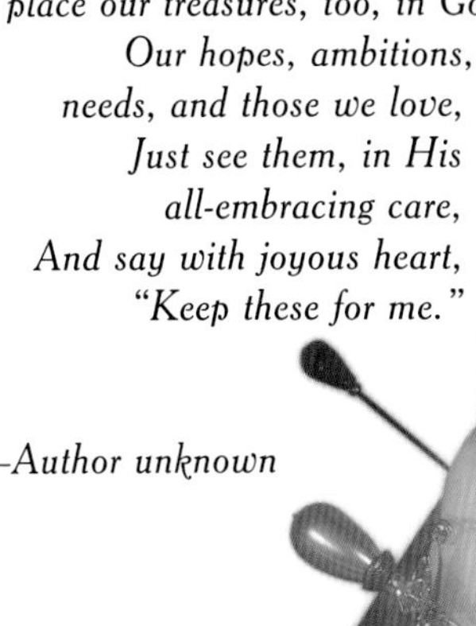

Learned by Heart

The Lord is my shepherd, I shall not want...Psalm 23:1

In his beautiful book, *I Shall Not Want,* Robert Ketchum tells of a Sunday school teacher who asked her group of children if anyone could quote the entire twenty-third psalm. A golden-haired four-and-a-half-year-old girl was among those who raised their hands. A bit skeptical, the teacher asked if she could really quote the entire psalm.

The little girl came to the rostrum, faced the class, made a perky little bow, and said: "The Lord is my shepherd, that's all I want." She bowed again and went and sat down.

That may well be the greatest interpretation I've ever heard.

—*Tim Hansel*
from You Gotta Keep Dancin'

Trust

Trust in the dark,
trust in the light,
trust at night
and trust in the morning,
and you will find that the faith
which may begin by mighty effort,
will end sooner or later
by becoming the easy and
natural habit of the soul.

—Hannah Whitall Smith
from *The Christian's Secret of a Happy Life*

The Angels Called It Good News

There came a time—at the best time, the right time—when the mighty Son of God turned His back on all the beauty and happiness of His forever home. And somehow—no one knows just how—He stepped out of Heaven and entered Earth as a baby.

It must have seemed a long way between Heaven and Earth.

It must have been sad to leave such a glorious home.

It must have made the angels wide-eyed and solemn to see the King they love and serve say good-bye and take that long step over the edge of Heaven—

—down

—down

—down

through black space to the little blue-and-brown planet where you and I live. Did the angels know that the man Jesus would have to die? Did they know that when He grew up His strong, gentle hands would be nailed to a cross of wood? Did they know their King would give up His life for all the wrong, hateful things you and I have done?

Did they know those things? I think they probably did.

But it wasn't long before they got to come to Earth, too. Late on a sleepy, star-sprinkled night, those angels peeled back the sky just like you would tear open a sparkling Christmas present. Then, with light and joy pouring our of Heaven like water through a broken dam, they began to shout and sing the message that baby Jesus had been born.

The world had a Savior! The angels called it "Good News," and it was.

It still is....

Larry Libby
from Someone Awesome

Now there were in the same country shepherds living out in the field, keeping watch over their flock by night. And behold, an angel of the Lord shone around them, and they were greatly afraid. Then the angel said to them, "Do not be afraid, for behold, I bring you good tidings of great joy which will be to all people. "For there is born to you this day in the city of David a Savior, who is Christ the Lord.

—Luke 2:8–11 NKJV

Our Greatest Need

If our greatest need had been knowledge,
God would have sent us an educator.
If our greatest need had been physical health,
God would have sent us a doctor.
If our greatest need had been money,
God would have sent us an entrepreneur.
If our greatest need had been excitement,
God would have sent us an entertainer.
But our greatest need was forgiveness,
so God send us a savior.

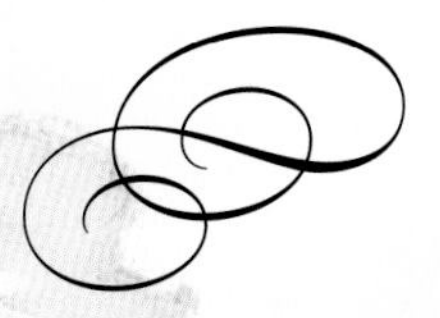

—Roy Lessin

One Solitary Life

He was born in an obscure village, the child of a peasant woman. He grew up in another village. He worked in a carpenter shop until he was thirty, and then for three years he was an itinerant preacher.

He never wrote a book.
He never held an office.
He never owned a home.
He never had a family.
He never went to college.

He never traveled more than two hundred miles from the place where he was born.

He never did any of the things that usually accompany greatness.

He had no credentials but himself.

While he was still a young man, the tide of public opinion turned against him. His friends ran away. He was turned over to his enemies and went through the mockery of a trial. He was nailed to a cross between two thieves. While he was dying, his executioners gambled for the only piece of property he had on earth, and that was his coat. When he was dead, he was laid in a borrowed grave through the kindness of a friend.

Nearly twenty centuries have come and gone, and today he is still the central figure of the human race and the leader of the mankind's progress.

I am far within the mark when I say that all the armies that have ever marched, all the navies that have ever sailed, all the parliaments that have ever sat, and all the kings that have ever reigned all put together, have not affected the life of man upon this earth as much as that One Solitary Life.

—Author unknown

Reference Point

One of the reference points of London is the Charing Cross. It is near the geographical center of the city and serves as a navigational tool for those confused by the streets.

A little girl was lost in the great city. A policeman found her. Between sobs and tears, she explained she didn't know her way home. He asked her if she knew her address. She didn't. He asked her phone number; she didn't know that either. But when he asked her what she knew, suddenly her face lit up.

"I know the Cross," she said. "Show me the Cross and I can find my way home from there."

—*Max Lucado*
from The Final Week of Jesus

Only Glimpses

Laurel knew she was dying. Over the weeks, we often talked about heaven—what it would look like and how it would be to live there. It seemed we always ended up crying and then holding each other tight in gentle hugs of hope.

The hardest part was trying to imagine something we had never seen, something about which we knew only a little.

And then I remembered this story—

The young girl with the blond hair and the deep blue eyes had been blind since birth. When she was twelve, the doctors were able to perform a new type of surgery that, if successful, would give her the gift of sight. The outcome would not be known for several days. After the bandages were removed, her eyes had to be protected from the light. So she sat in darkness, waiting.

The mother spent long hours answering her daughter's questions about what things looked like and what she should expect. They were both so excited about the possibility of being able to see that neither of them slept much. Over and over, even in the darkness, they talked about every lovely thing they could imagine—colors, shapes, beauty of every kind.

Finally the moment came when the young girl's eyes could endure enough light for her to look out the window. She stood there for a long time without saying a word. Outside, the spring day was ideal, bright and warm with fluffy white clouds decorating the blue sky. Lacy blossoms sprinkled to the ground like pink snow as soft breezes stirred the cherry trees. Yellow crocuses proudly lined the brick walkway that wound across the grass.

When the girl turned back to her mother, tears were streaming down her cheeks. "Oh, Mother. Why didn't you tell me it would be so beautiful?"

I shared this story with my friend, tears filling my own eyes: "Laurel, right now we're sitting in the darkness, but before long you will be asking God the same question about heaven."

—Alice Gray
from More Stories for the Heart

Heaven

Think of—
Stepping on shore,
and finding it Heaven!
Of taking hold of a hand,
and finding it God's hand.
Of breathing a new air,
and finding it celestial air.
Of feeling invigorated,
and finding it immortality.
Of passing from storm to
tempest to an unbroken calm.
Of waking up,
and finding it Home.

—Author Unknown

OTHER BOOKS COMPILED BY ALICE GRAY

• *Stories for the Heart* • *More Stories for the Heart* • *Christmas Stories for the Heart* • *Stories for the Family's Heart* • *Stories for a Woman's Heart* • *Stories for a Man's Heart* • *Keepsakes for the Heart - Mother* • *Keepsakes for the Heart - Friendship* • *Keepsakes for the Heart - Love*

KEEPSAKES FOR THE HEART—FAITH
published by Multnomah Publishers, Inc.

International Standard Book Number: 1-57673-564-8

Cover and interior design by Stephen Gardner.
Printed in China

For information:
MULTNOMAH PUBLISHERS, INC.
POST OFFICE BOX 1720
SISTERS, OREGON 97759

99 00 01 02 03—7 6 5 4 3 2 1

ACKNOWLEDGEMENTS

Grateful acknowledgement is given to all who have contributed to this book. Any inadvertent omissions of credit will be gladly corrected in future editions.

"Come Home!" by Billy Graham from *Unto the Hills* (Nashville, TN, Word Publishing, ©1991). Used with permission. All rights reserved.

"Even If It's Dark" by Ron Mehl from *God Works the Night Shift* (Sisters, OR, Multnomah Publishers, Inc., ©1994). Used with permission.

"No Wasted Pieces" by Gigi Graham Tchividjian from *Currents of the Heart* (Sisters, OR, Multnomah Publishers, Inc., ©1996). Used with permission.

"The Treasure" by Alice Gray from *More Stories for the Heart* (Sisters, OR, Multnomah Publishers, Inc., ©1997). Used with permission.

"The Father's Pleasure" by Robin Jones Gunn from *Mothering By Heart* (Sisters, OR, Multnomah Publishers, Inc., ©1996). Used with permission.

"Drifting" by Tony Evans, President, The Urban Alternative. Used with permission.

"Morning Song" by Ruth Bell Graham from *Legacy of a Pack Rat* (Nashville, TN, Thomas Nelson Publishers, ©1989). Used with permission of the author.

"Learned by Heart" by Tim Hansel from *You Gotta Keep Dancin'* (Colorado Springs, CO, David C. Cook Publishing Co., ©1985). Used with permission.

"The Angels Called It Good News" by Larry Libby from *Someone Awesome* (Sisters, OR, Gold 'n' Honey Books, Multnomah Publishers, Inc., ©1995). Used with permission.

"Our Greatest Need" by Roy Lessin. Used with permission of DaySpring Cards. All rights reserved.

"Reference Point" by Max Lucado from *The Final Week of Jesus* (Sisters, OR, Multnomah Publishers, Inc., ©1994). Used with permission.

"Only Glimpses" by Alice Gray from *More Stories for the Heart* (Sisters, OR, Multnomah Publishers, Inc., ©1997). Used with permission.